CFA 2026 level 1: Portfolio management

CFA level 1

M. Imran Ahsan

Published by M. Imran Ahsan, 2025.

CFA 2026 LEVEL 1: PORTFOLIO MANAGEMENT

First edition. September 11, 2025.

ISBN: 979-8232300937

Written by M. Imran Ahsan.

Also by M. Imran Ahsan

ACCA

ACCA: Business & Technology

CFA level 1

CFA 2026: Level 1 corporate Issuers

CFA 2026: Level 1 Financial Statement Analysis

CFA level 1: 2026 Equity Investments

CFA 2026 LEVEL 1: Economics

CFA 2026 Level 1: Derivatives and Alternative Investments

CFA 2026 level 1: Portfolio management

Investment series

Corporate Finance: A Beginner's Guide

Fixed Income Securities: A Beginner's Guide to Understand, Invest and Evaluate Fixed Income Securities

Personal Finance

Side Hustle Success: Unlock Your Earning Potential

Table of Contents

CFA 2026 level 1: Portfolio management (CFA level 1) 1

Learning Module 1 | Portfolio Risk and Return: Part I 2

Learning Module 2 | Portfolio Risk and Return: Part II 12

Learning Module 3 | Portfolio Management: An Overview............ 23

Learning Module 4 | Basics of Portfolio Planning and Construction 35

Learning module 5 | The Behavioral Biases of Individuals 42

Leaning Module 6 | Introduction to Risk Management 54

To all smart learners

"The most important quality for an investor is temperament, not intellect." -

Warren Buffett

CFA level 1, 2026

Portfolio management

Complete portfolio management in just one week

By

M. Imran Ahsan

Learning Module 1
Portfolio Risk and Return: Part I

1: Describe characteristics of the major asset classes that investors consider in forming portfolios

Investors always have a choice; they can either choose to invest in lower risk lower return assets or in higher risk with higher return assets. There is always risk-return trade off.

Historic data of USA financial market suggests following

Asset class	Expected average return	Risk (standard deviation)	Liquidity
Large cap stocks	Lower than Small cap stocks	Lower than Small cap stocks	Higher than Small cap stocks
Small cap stocks	Higher than large cap stocks	Higher than large cap stocks	Lower than large cap stocks
Long-term corporate bonds	Lower than Small and large cap stocks	Lower than Small and large cap stocks	Depends on credibility
Long-term government bonds	Lower than small cap, large cap stocks and Long-term corporate bonds	Higher than Long-term corporate bonds but lower than large and small cap stocks	Higher
Treasury bills	Lower than all above	Lower than all above	Highest than all of above

2: Explain risk aversion and its implications for portfolio selection

Risk aversion: In portfolio theory it is assumed that the investors are risk averse. They prefer less risky investment over a more risky investment if the outcomes are same or even less. It may also suggest that a risk averse investor gets highest utility when he invests in least risky assets.

Risk seeking: If an investor is risk seeking, it means she love to take risk and prefers more risk over less risk. A gambling behavior is risk seeking behavior. It may also suggest that the risk seeker gets highest utility when he invests in high risk assets with highest expected returns.

Risk neutral: Risk neutral behavior means the investor is indifferent about risk. It may also suggest that the risk neutral investor will get highest utility when he invests in highest return generating security (off course with highest risk).

For example there are two investments with same initial cost but one will definitely generate $ 50 while other can generate $70 inflow or 50$ loss. The risk averse investor will chose the investment which will certainly generate $50 while risk seeker investor tends to chose second investment. A risk neutral can chose any investment (or he can choose second security because it can produce higher return).

3: Explain the selection of an optimal portfolio, given an investor's utility (or risk aversion) and the capital allocation line

Utility: Utility is the quality of anything which can satisfy a human want. In simple words we can say utility is the satisfaction.

Indifference curve: Indifference curve is the combination of all portfolios which gives same level of satisfaction. According to indifference curve approach, utility cannot be measured but we can rank it as higher level of utility and lower level of utility.

Higher Indifference curve (IC) shows higher utility while lower IC shows lower level of utility.

When we combine utility with portfolio management we can express it as follows;

$$U = E(R) - \frac{1}{2}(A\sigma^2)$$

Whereas

U is the utility level of an investment

E(R) is the expected return

A is risk aversion coefficient

σ^2 is portfolio variance

A is the additional reward an investor want in order to accept additional risk so, “A” would be higher for more risk averse investor

”A” would be lower for less risk averse investor

“A” will be zero for risk neutral investor. The utility of risk neutral investor only depends on level of E(R)

And “A” will be negative for risk lover.

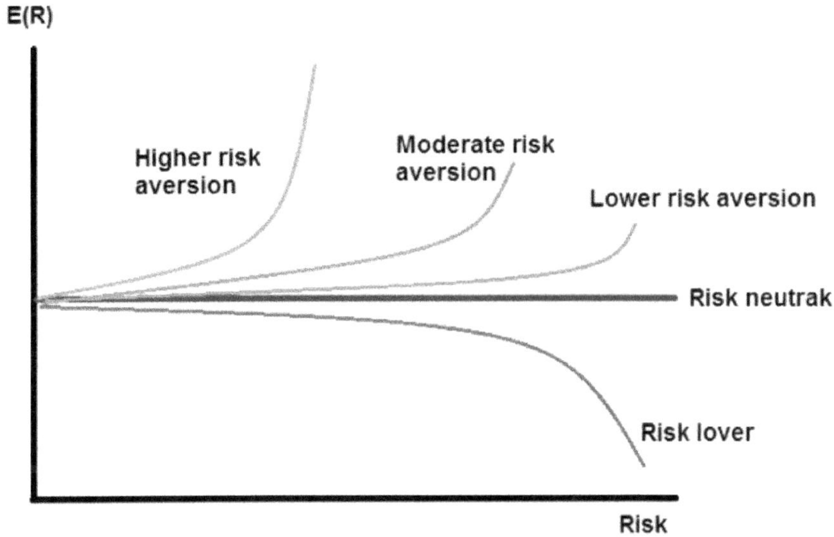

We can see from above figure that, an investor who hates risk has steeper indifference curve because she needs higher reward for one unit of additional risk.

Capital allocation line: The two fund separation theorem states that the optimal portfolio of any investor must have risk free and risky assets.

Capital allocation line shows the risk of risk free assets and risky assets. It is created by combining all possible combinations of risky and risk free assets. It shows the expected return which an investor might earn by assuming certain level of risk. The slope of CAL is the trade-off between risk and return.

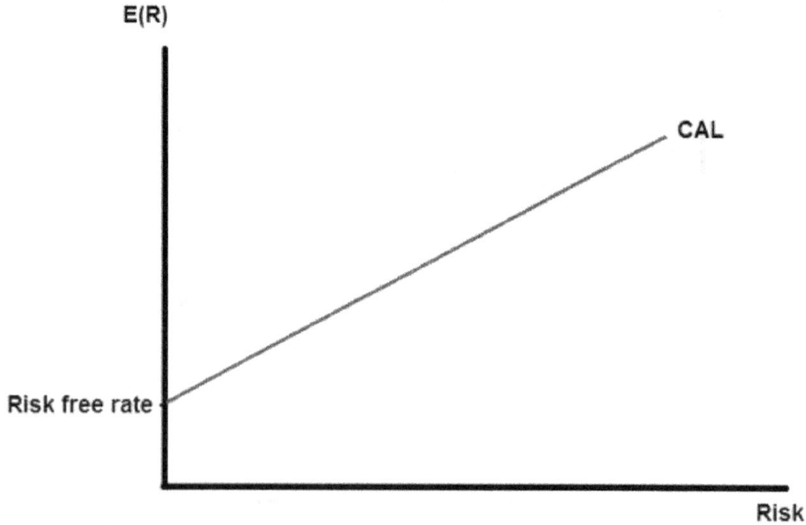

Combining IC and CAL

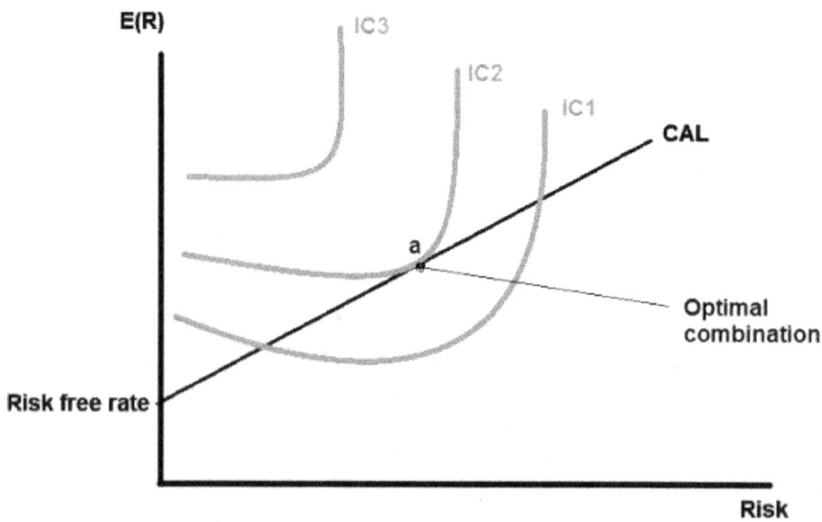

At point "a" of IC2 is the highest level of utility which an investor can gain given all these ICs and CAL. IC3 is not attainable while IC1 is not optimal as the investor can increase her utility level by going to IC2 and attain extra return with same level of risk.

4: Calculate and interpret the mean, variance, and covariance (or correlation) of asset returns based on historical data

In finance, mean is used to estimate expected return, variance and standard deviation are calculated using mean to measure investment risk while covariance and correlation are used to measure the relationship between two securities.

All these measures are calculated using historical data.

Mean/Arithmetic mean/Average return/Mean return: This is also a simple and easy to calculate measure. It can be used for multiple periods. We can use it to calculate average return of different periods (we can use average of holding period returns). Arithmetic mean is upward biased. It means it will give us higher average return if holding periods are not same.

Formula

$$AM = \sum \frac{xi}{n}$$

Whereas

AM is Arithmetic mean

Xi is the total return in period i

N is total number of returns

Variance: It is a measure of dispersion from mean value to calculate risk. A population variance can be calculated as;

$$\text{Variance } (\sigma^2) = \{ \textstyle\sum_{i=1}^{N} (Xi - \mu)^2 \} \div N$$

Whereas

σ^2 is population variance

Xi is individual observation

μ is population mean

N is population size.

Sample variance is same as population variance except it is not calculated using whole population (we use a sample size to calculate it).

Sample variance S^2 can be calculated as

$$S^2 = \{ \sum_{i=1}^{n} (Xi - \bar{X})^2 \} \div n - 1$$

Whereas;

X is sample mean

\`n\` is sample size

Standard deviation is the "square root of variance"

Covariance: Covariance measures how two variables (expected returns in case of portfolio) move together over time.

Sample covariance can be calculated between two variables x and y as;

$$\sigma x,y = \frac{\sum_{i=1}^{n} (Xi-x)(Yi-\bar{y})(Xi-x)}{n-1}$$

Whereas

Xi is individual observation of variable x

$\bar{x}$ is mean of x variable values

Yi are individual observations of Y variable

$\bar{y}$ is the mean value of Y.

n is the sample size

The value of covariance depends on individual values we use and relationship between variables. A positive covariance means two variables tend to move in same direction. A negative covariance means they tend to move in opposite direction. A Zero covariance means they have no historic relationship. Covariance is an absolute measure and its magnitude does not tell us much. A more standardized measure is correlation.

Correlation: Correlation tells us the strength of relationship between two variables.

Correlation between two variables can be calculated as;

corr(X,Y) = Covariance / $\sigma x^{*}\sigma y$

σx means standard deviation of x.

σy means standard deviation of y.

+1 correlation means two variables perfectly move in same direction.

-1 correlation means two variables perfectly move in opposite direction.

'0' correlation means two variables are perfectly uncorrelated.

5: Calculate and interpret portfolio standard deviation

Let's assume we have two securities (X and Y) in our portfolio. The total risk of our portfolio is not the sum of risks of individual securities as there is covariance involved. Total risk can be less than or maximum equal to sum of individual risks of comprising securities.

Portfolio variance = $(Wx)^2 (\sigma x) + (Wy)^2 (\sigma Y) + 2WxWy\ \sigma x\ \sigma Y\ \rho xy$

Whereas

Wx is the weight of security X in portfolio

Wy is the weight of security Y in portfolio

σx is the SD of X

σy is the SD of Y

ρxy is the correlation coefficient of X and Y.

Now we know that standard deviation is square root

Portfolio standard deviation =$\sqrt{[}(Wx)^2 (\sigma x) + (Wy)^2 (\sigma Y) + 2WxWy\ \sigma x\ \sigma Y\ \rho xy]$

$\sigma x\ \sigma Y\ \rho xy$ is the covariance of X ad Y. This result can be derived from following previously used equation

ρ (X,Y) = Covariance / $\sigma x^{*}\sigma y$

6: Describe the effect on a portfolio's risk of investing in assets that are less than perfectly correlated

The total risk of our portfolio is not the sum of risks of individual securities as there is covariance involved. Total risk can be less than or maximum equal to sum of individual risks of comprising securities.

If two Securities have -1 correlation (perfectly negative correlation) and their proportion is same in a portfolio, there would be zero investment risk. If one security rises the other will fall with same proportion. If they are perfectly positive correlated (+1correlation coefficient) the total risk is simply the sum of individual risks of each security.

Having a correlation between +1 and -1 is called less than perfect correlation. In this case the overall risk of a portfolio is less than sum of individual risks of each security.

7: Describe and interpret the minimum-variance and efficient frontiers of risky assets and the global minimum-variance portfolio

In finance theory we assume that the investors are risk averse. They do not like risks and want to minimize it. Investors have to find investable securities which are least risky with a given level of expected return. When we make a graph of all these securities, that is called efficient frontier or minimum variance frontier. The portion of efficient frontier where there are least risky portfolios reside is called global minimum-variance portfolio.

To make efficient frontier we select all the securities with minimum variance and given level of return. A rational investor must choose between all those portfolios which are on efficient frontier because they are least risky given the expected return.

All other portfolios or securities are more risky.

Note: Here we are ignoring the securities which have zero investment risk (like government issued securities).

Minimum Variance frontier

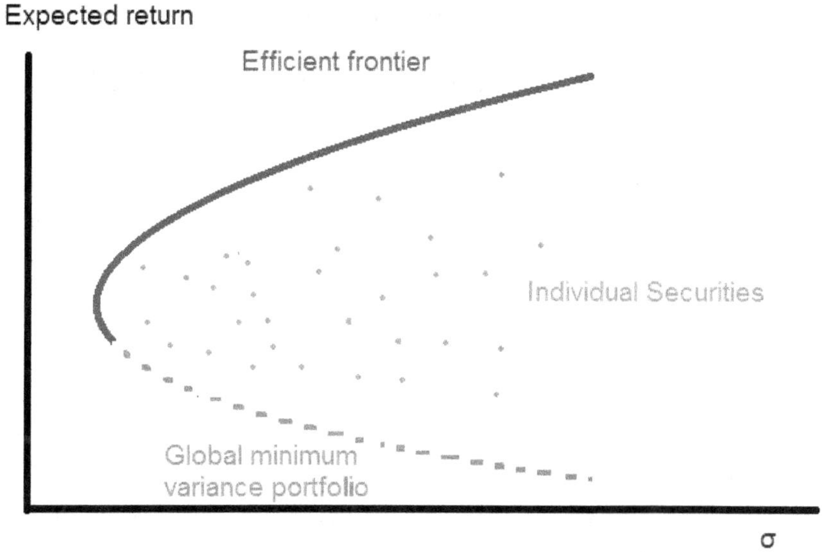

Learning Module 2
Portfolio Risk and Return: Part II

1: Describe the implications of combining a risk-free asset with a portfolio of risky

Assets

An investor can improve risk and rerun of a portfolio by combining risky and risk-free assets in her portfolio. The expected return of portfolio depends on weights of risk free assets and risky assets in portfolio and their correlation.

If the assets are less than perfectly correlated, the total risk of portfolio is less than their sum of individual risks.

$E(R_p) = W_{rf}E(R_{rf}) + W_bE(R_b)$

$E(R_p)$ is the expected return of portfolio

W_{rf} is the weight of risk free asset

$E(R_{rf})$ is the expected return of risk free asset

W_b is the weight of risky asset

$E(R_b)$ is the expected return of risky asset

While the portfolio risk is

Portfolio standard deviation $=\sqrt{[(Wrf)^2(\sigma rf) + (Wb)^2(\sigma b) + 2Wrf\,Wb\,\sigma rf\,\sigma b\,\rho rf.b]}$

Whereas

$\sigma rf\,\sigma b \rho rf.b$ is the covariance of risky and risk free assets.

2: Explain the capital allocation line (CAL) and the capital market line (CML)

Capital allocation line: The two fund separation theorem states that the optimal portfolio of any investor must have risk free and risky assets.

Capital allocation line shows the risk of risk free assets and risky assets. It is created by combining all possible combinations of risky and risk free assets. It shows the expected return which an investor might earn by assuming certain level of risk. The slope of CAL is the trade-off between risk and return, $(\mathbf{R_p} - \mathbf{R_{rf}}) / \sigma_p$ (also known as Sharpe ratio).

Rp is portfolio return

Rrf is risk free rate

σp is portfolio standard deviation.

We will discuss Sharpe ratio in LOS 53i.

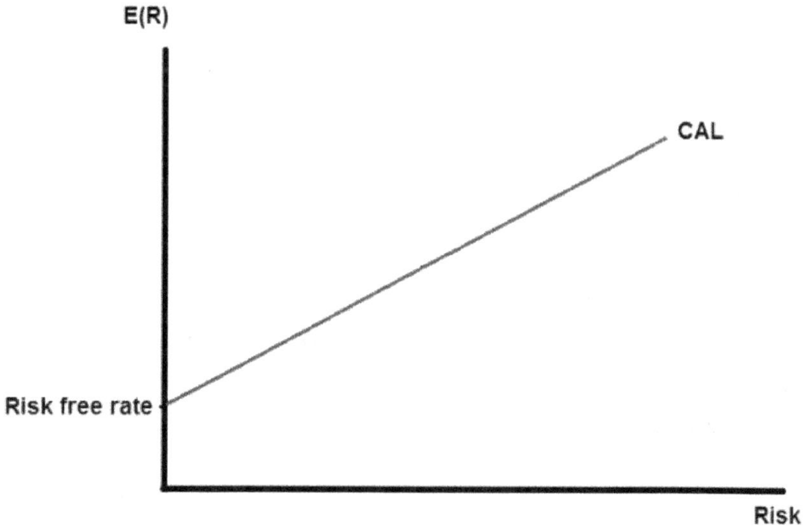

Capital market line (CML): CML is the special case of CAL where the risk-portfolio is the market portfolio.

If for all investors, the expected risk and return characteristics of risk-assets are homogeneous, then all the investors will choose a portfolio of risk-assets on CML which is tangent to efficient frontier.

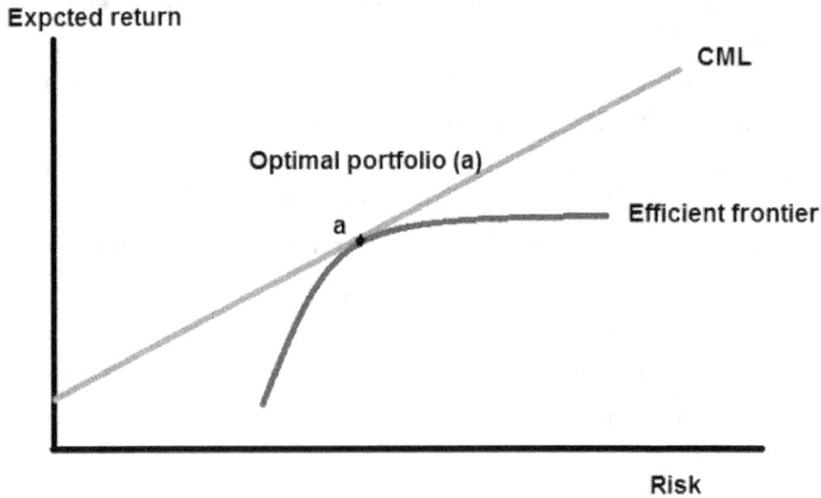

Here optimal risk portfolio is the market portfolio.

In practice, the expected risk and return for all investors is different and they choose different portfolios depending on their risk tolerance and desired return (depend on their IC). Some investors go up alongside of CML or CAL to have higher expected return with extra risk.

3: Explain systematic and nonsystematic risk, including why an investor should not

expect to receive additional return for bearing nonsystematic risk

Nonsystematic risk: The risk attached to a specific security which can be avoided by diversification is called nonsystematic risk. In portfolio theory the nonsystematic risk can be avoided because diversification is free or cost of diversification is extremely low. For example we can hold securities with less perfect correlation or we can buy stocks of a mutual fund which is diversified by professionals.

Systematic or market risk: The risk which exists with the market and cannot be avoided is called systematic or market risk. This risk is attached with the overall market and depends on overall economic variables like GDP growth, interest rate other crisis etc.

Portfolio theory states that as we buy more and more different securities we can diversify our portfolio and the additional risk reduces. Some studies states that holding 30 different stocks reduces nonsystematic risk almost close to zero. So, the investors are only rewarded for taking systematic risk.

4: Explain return generating models (including the market model) and their uses

Return generating models are used to estimate returns of different securities using different input variables. The most general model which uses almost all affecting variables (like inflation, interest rate, company fundamentals etc) is multifactor model. Multifactor model can be used to estimate the intrinsic value of a single security or a portfolio. The general form of multifactor model is as follows;

$$R_i = E(R_i) + \beta_{i1}F1 + \beta_{i2}F2 + \beta_{i3}F3 \ldots\ldots\ldots\ldots \beta_{in}F_n + \varepsilon$$

Whereas

Ri is the return on asset 'i' or portfolio 'i'.

E(Ri) is the expected return on asset 'i' or portfolio 'i'.

$\beta i1$ is the sensitivity of stock i to the factor 1.

F1 is the first factor that can affect return on asset i.

$\beta i2$ is the sensitivity of stock i to the factor 2

F2 the second factor that can affect return on asset i

βin the sensitivity of stock i to the factor n.

ε is statistical error. It is the return unexplained by any factor.

We can use factors like change in GDP, interest rate, company`s revenues changes etc.

The multifactor model is often expressed in risky minus risk free return as;

$$R_i - R_f = E(R_i) + \beta_{i1}F1 + \beta_{i2}F2 + \beta_{i3}F3 \ldots\ldots\ldots\ldots \beta_{in}F_n + \varepsilon$$

Rf is the risk free rate.

It tells us that the excessive return from risk free rate is dependent on all the factors which we will include in our mode.

Fama and French three factor model: It uses three factors to which expected return is sensitive to. These factors are; Size of firm (small minus big (SMB), Book value to market (high minus low, HML) and excessive return on market portfolio from risk free return ($R_m - R_{rf}$).

$\mathbf{R_i - R_{rf} = \alpha_i + \beta_{SMB}(SMB) + \beta_{HML}(HML) + \beta_{SMB}(SMB) + \beta_M(R_m - R_{rf}) + \varepsilon}$

This model considers that the small cap value stocks generally outperform the market. This model adjusts the risk factor of these elements.

Single factor model/Single-index model: It is the single factor form of above mentioned model which uses single factor (the market portfolio return).

$\mathbf{R_i - R_{rf} = \beta_M(R_m - R_{rf}) + \varepsilon}$

Market model:

$\mathbf{R_i = \alpha_i + \beta_i(R_m - R_{rf}) + \varepsilon}$

Here $\mathbf{R_m}$ is the market index return.

5: Calculate and interpret beta

Beta is the risk of a specific security in relation with market risk. Beta is the sensitivity of security`s return to the market index. It measures the systematic risk and its value depends on the correlation between security and the whole market (or index).

βi = Cov (Ri, Rm) ÷ Variance(m)

Cov (Ri, Rm) is the covariance of a specific security and market. It tells us how these two move together. A positive covariance tells us that they move in same direction while negative covariance tells us they move in opposite direction

Variance (m) is the market variance around mean. By definition the beta of market is one so

$\beta i < 1$ it means the security is less risk than market

$\beta i > 1$ it means the security is riskier than market

If Beta is zero it is most likely the risk free security. If the security and the market have no correlation, it can also produce zero beta and that does not necessarily mean the security is a risk free security.

(We must take absolute values)

A positive beta also means that the security `i` and the market moves in same direction while negative beta shows movement in opposite direction.

6: Explain the capital asset pricing model (CAPM), including its assumptions, and the security market line (SML)

7: Calculate and interpret the expected return of an asset using the CAPM

CAPM: CAPM is a widely used model to evaluate the expected return of a security given its risk. It describes relationship between expected return of a security and its systematic risk beta.

CAPM formula

$E(Ri) = Rrf + \beta i\{E(Rm) - Rrf\}$

E (Ri) is expected return on a security

Rrf is risk free rate

βi is the beta of security i.

$\{E(Rm) - Rrf\}$ is the risk premium

Assumptions of CAPM

1. Investors are risk averse. They use diversification to reduce risk.
2. Investors want to maximize their utility. They will choose portfolio according to their utility preferences (on the basis of risk and return characteristics).
3. All the investors have homogeneous expectations about

expected return, risk and correlations (that's a very strong assumption)

4. All investors have same time horizons.
5. All investors have free access to all available information
6. The markets are frictionless. It means there are no trading costs, no taxes and no any other restrictions on trading.
7. All securities are infinitely divisible. One investor can invest in any amount of securities.
8. No investor can influence the market.

Security market line (SML): SML is the graphical representation of CAPM. As we use beta in CAPM so in x-axis of SML we have beta for risk (in opposed to CAL where we use total risk on x-axis).

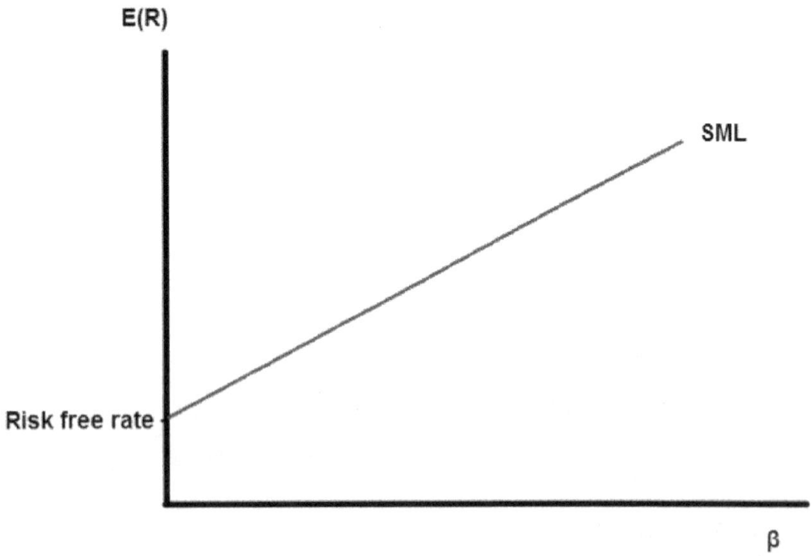

The CAL represents all possible efficient portfolios but SML shows all securities (weather efficient or not). The slope of SML is {E(Rm) – Rrf} is the risk premium. We know that for efficient portfolio total risk is only the systematic risk.

While

$\beta i = Cov\ (Ri, Rm) \div Variance(m)$

8: Describe and demonstrate applications of the CAPM and the SML

CAPM and SML are widely used for pricing of securities and performance evaluation given its systematic risk. Its calculations are very simple.

Comparison: CAPM can be used to compare risk and return of different securities and an investor can invest intelligently.

This model also helps to construct a diversified portfolio.

With the help of SML we can easily select undervalued securities and sale overvalued securities.

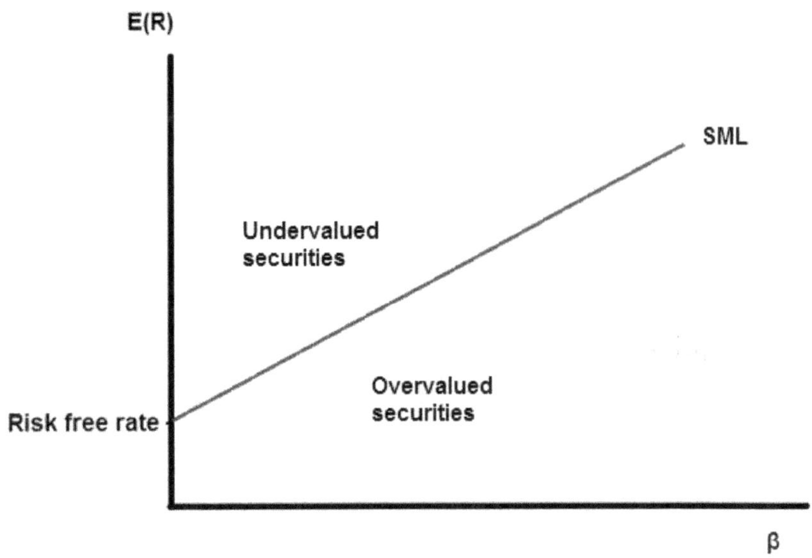

The securities above the SML are undervalued for the given risk and therefore are good buy. The securities under the SML are overvalued and can be sold.

9: Calculate and interpret the Sharpe ratio, Treynor ratio, M2, and Jensen's alpha

The sharp ratio, Treynor ratio, M2 and Jensen`s alpha are risk adjusted return measures.

These measures are used to compare different portfolios that have different risks.

Sharpe ratio: Sharpe ratio is the risk premium divided by portfolio risk. Here we use total risk. It is the excessive return per unit of total risk.

Sharpe ratio= $(R_p - R_{rf}) / \sigma_p$

Whereas

Rp is portfolio return

Rrf is risk free rate

σp is portfolio standard deviation (Total risk).

$(R_p - R_{rf})$ is also called portfolio risk premium.

A portfolio with higher Sharpe ratio is better as it will generate higher risk adjusted returns. Value of Sharpe ratio itself does not tells us anything. It is used to rank different portfolios. Sharpe ratio can help an investor to examine whether the higher returns are due to better investment decisions or due to extra risk exposure.

Limitations of Sharpe ratio: A negative Sharpe ratio either means that the risk free rate is higher than portfolio return or the portfolio is generating negative returns.

Sharpe ratio can also be easily manipulated. The investment manager can use annualized standard deviation or can use standard deviation of most stable period in order to generate higher Sharpe ratio.

Treynor ratio: It is just like Sharpe ratio but we use systematic risk instead of total risk.

Treynor ratio = $(R_p - R_{rf}) / \beta_p$

It is the excessive risk on portfolio per unit of systematic risk.

βp is the systematic risk.

A portfolio with higher Treynor ratio is better than another portfolio with lower Treynor ratio because portfolio with higher Treynor ratio will generate better return per unit of systematic risk.

Use of systematic risk is the benefit of this ratio because beta cannot be easily manipulated. Beta also makes more sense as the unsystematic risk can be easily avoided by diversification.

A negative Treynor ratio is meaningless.

Modigliani- Modigliani risk adjusted performance or M-Squared ratio (M^2)**:** It is derived from Sharpe ratio but M^2 gives result in percentage form which is an advantage of this measure.

The intuition behind this measure is that we create a portfolio 'P' that mimics the risk of market or an index.

$$M^2 = (R_p - R_{rf})\frac{\sigma_m}{\sigma_p} - (R_m - R_{rf})$$

R_p is the return on our portfolio

R_{rf} is the risk free rate of return

R_m is the market rate of return

σ_m is the market standard deviation

σ_p is the standard deviation of our portfolio

$\frac{\sigma_m}{\sigma_p}$ is the weight of our portfolio in relative to market.

M^2 is also used to rank different investments.

M^2 =0 means out portfolio will produce market rate of return

M^2 >0 means our portfolio will outperform the market

M^2 <0 means our portfolio will generate fewer return compare with the market.

Jensen`s Alpha: It is also a risk adjusted measure. It measures the excessive returns of a portfolio over or below than predicted by CAPM.

Formula

$$\alpha_p = Rp - [Rrf + \beta p\,(Rm - Rrf)$$

αp is Jensen`s alpha for our portfolio.

If the Jensen`s alpha is positive, our portfolio have beaten the market (earned more than required rate of return).

If the Jensen`s alpha is negative, out portfolio have not generated the required rate of return and performed poor than market.

If the Jensen`s alpha is zero it might indicate that our portfolio is perfectly tracking market or an index and producing same return as the market is.

Learning Module 3
Portfolio Management: An Overview

1: Describe the portfolio approach to investing

Portfolio means collection of different investments by individual investors or institutions in order to reduce investment risk. Different investments include holding stocks of different companies, bonds, real estate etc. The process of holding different types of investment at same time is called diversification.

When an investor holds a single security, she is not diversifying her investment. It means if the security price fall, all of her investment will go down. On the other hand holding a lot of securities reduce risk because some securities will fall while others will rise with the passage of time. There is a famous quote "Do not put all your eggs into a single basket".

An investor must try to hold the securities with highest negative correlation. "-1" is the ideal correlation for portfolio diversification. If two securities have -1 correlation, it means they move in opposite direction and it's a 100 % hedge against risk. Investors should focus on the correlation between the securities within portfolio because the correlation can change over time.

Always remember portfolio diversification is hedge against market risk in normal market conditions. In an era of market turmoil, generally all securities prices fall. This phenomenon is called contagion (for example (2008 crisis).

2: Describe the steps in the portfolio management process

There are three steps in portfolio management process;

1. Planning
2. Execution

3. Feedback

1. **Planning:** In this step we analyze client's investment goal, time horizon, risk tolerance, liquidity needs, tax and other obligations and other circumstances which can affect her investment. After the analysis we write IPS (Investment policy statement). IPS contains investment objectives, constraints and a related benchmark to compare portfolio`s performance. This statement can be and should be updated as soon as investor`s circumstances change.

1. **Execution:** In this step we do following; Asset allocation, security analysis and construct portfolio according to IPS. It means we (as an analyst) analyze risk and return characteristics of different securities and allocate the client's funds and develop a portfolio. The resultant portfolio must match the risk tolerance and return goals of the investor.

The analyst use top-down analysis for the asset allocation. It may include over all macroeconomic conditions like GDP growth rate, inflation rate, interest rate etc. After that, bottom-up analysis is done by examining attractive and under-valuated securities. We can develop portfolio containing stocks, fixed income private and government securities.

1. **Feedback:** Once the portfolio is developed, it must be monitored and rebalanced after intervals or whenever the investor`s or overall macroeconomic circumstances changes. For example if a security`s risk characteristics increases we should eliminate and replace it with another security with less risk characteristic. The portfolio must be monitored evaluated with respect to benchmark and reported to client.

3: Describe types of investors and distinctive characteristics and needs of each

The need and characteristics of every investor can vary but we can group them into two broad categories: the individual investors and institutional investors.

1. **Individual Investors:** Individual investors can have short term or long term goals. For example plan to buy a house or children's education can be a short term goal while plan for retirement pension is a long term goal. Some individual investors look for fixed income generating opportunities while others want capital appreciation and or deferment of taxes. Some individual investors are retail investors while others can be "high-net-worth investors. Their investment goals can also depend on their financial position, employment and other obligations so does their risk tolerance.

1. **Institutional Investors:** Institutional investors can also have long term and or short term investment goals. Usually institutional investors are the major participants in financial market. Institutional investors can be following;

Banks: Usually the banks have short term investment goals. They want to earn extra on excessive reserves. They usually invest in liquid assets like money market instruments so they can quickly withdraw funds to fulfill depositors' claims.

Insurance companies: Insurance companies sell insurance products and receive premiums. They need to invest so that they have sufficient funds to fulfill insurance claims. Some insurance companies like life- insurance have long term objectives while property and loss insurance companies have shorter time horizons.

Investment companies: Investment companies need to invest a pool of funds in different securities in order to earn for their financers. Time horizon of different investment companies differ with respect to their investment goals. Some companies use conservative approach to save principal amount while earning. Some companies use aggressive investment approach to earn extra.

Endowment funds: Endowment funds can invest in a way to maintain principal amount (inflation adjusted) while earning a rate of return to fund some ongoing projects like educational and or general welfare projects. Usually the time horizon of these funds is longer.

Foundations: Foundations are charitable institutions which are established for the welfare of a particular region, people or to support other welfare projects like creating a vaccine for a specific disease. The investment time horizon of a foundation can be the same as endowment fund because it also has to save original amount (inflation adjusted) while funding some ongoing project. Usually the time horizon of foundations is longer.

Sovereign investment fund: It is the investment company owned by government. These funds invest excessive government funds to earn and to maintain principal amount (inflation adjusted).

4: Describe defined contribution and defined benefit pension plans

Pension: It is the amount of funds collected from employees during their services. These funds are used to support the person after retirement.

The two broad categories of pension plan are defined contribution plan and defined pension plan.

Defined contribution plan: It is a retirement plan in which employer contributes a certain amount of money in each period (i.e. monthly) into employee`s retirement account. The contribution may depend on employee`s contribution, employee`s experience, duration of employee`s services etc. The employee can also contribute same or different amount. The firm provides no promises about the future value of the plan. The money is invested and it can earn positive or negative earnings. The investment decisions are left to employee. The employee bears all the risks involved linked to investment.

Financial reporting requirement: Financial reporting requirements for defined contribution plan are straight forward. Amount contributed by employer is his pension expense and there is no future liability to report on balance sheet.

Defined benefit plan: It is a retirement plan in which the employer assumes risk of future value of the plan. The employer promises to pay certain periodic payments to employee in future (after retirement). In this plan the employer contributes certain amount (the employee may or may not contribute) into fund. The employer generally sends the amount to an institution which is specialized for investment. The employer makes sure a certain future value of the fund. The retirement benefits usually depend on employee`s years of service, or the compensations at retirement. For example, an employee who is to be entitled 3% of her salary (0f $200000) and served for 30 years may get

200000 x 30 x 2% = $120000

Financial reporting requirement: Financial reporting is complicated here. The employer needs to estimate value of future obligation of defined benefit plan. The variables used to forecast are mortality rate, future compensation amount (salary), retirement age and discount rate.

5: Describe aspects of the asset management industry

Asset management industry is a collection of all firms who deal with investment assets.

Asset management industry can include "buy-side and sell-side firms, Active or passive managers, Traditional or alternative form of investment firms etc.

Buy side vs sell side: Usually when we talk about asset management firms, we mean buy-side firms. These firms buy investment product for their clients and help them to achieve their financial goals.

Buy-side can include retail investors, high-net-worth investors, institutional investors, mutual funds, private equity funds, pension funds etc. on the other hand sell-side firms include all those firms who sell investment products like commercial and investment banks and brokers.

Active vs passive management firms: Active investment managers try to beat the benchmark and are expected to earn more than passive management firms. Active managers use aggressive strategies to achieve their goal. Passive managers just try to replicate benchmark.

Conventional/traditional vs alternative investment management: Traditional investment means investment in common, preferred stocks and or bonds and to create diversified portfolio.

Alternative investment managers invest directly or indirectly in derivatives, real estate private equity etc. A new trend is being emerged that the conventional investment managers are also taking part in alternative investments to diversify their portfolios.

Latest trends in asset management industry.

Lately the investors are moving towards passive investment because the fee is very low and also because the active management is not producing (or at least it seems to) much excessive returns due to highly efficient markets. When the markets are efficient they quickly adjust to new information and there is little room for the profitable transactions.

Different types of modern software are being used to analyze huge amount of data (big data) (using different models and algorithms to predict future more accurately. They analyze the date in a quick way.

Managers who use these techniques will be able to predict and exploit any opportunity and can involve in short term trading.

Robo-advisors are digital platforms that provide automated financial services to investors with little or even without human involvement. These advisors are efficient and charge lowest fee.

6: Describe mutual funds and compare them with other pooled investment products

Pooled investments are the investment vehicles which deal with different investments. These vehicles include mutual funds, exchange traded funds, hedge funds and asset backed securities.

Mutual funds

Mutual funds hold the securities of other companies. The investors can buy the securities of these funds directly from the funds (open end funds) or from existing investors (closed end funds). Buying securities of a mutual fund is an alternative of having a portfolio. This is because the mutual funds hold diversified portfolio of securities. Investors can invest in mutual funds with generally low minimum investment. These funds are evaluated by NAV (net asset value). Net asset value is determined at closing price of underlying securities held by that fund in portfolio.

Open-end mutual fund: As the name shows, these funds always accept new funds from investors. The investors can purchase units of these mutual funds at NAV at the time of investment. The investors can also withdraw their funds at NAV at time of withdrawal minus fee and other charges. The managers of these funds have to continuously search for new securities for new inflow of funds and to manage cash for withdrawals. That's why they charge higher fee usually for withdrawals. Due to continuous inflows and outflows, total numbers of shares of these funds continuously change. Inflow of cash can also create opportunities for open end funds to grow. The dividend income is used to purchase extra units of open end mutual funds (the managers offer existing investors to buy extra units of mutual funds with dividend income).

Closed-end mutual funds: The share of closed-end mutual funds is lower in mutual fund industry. These funds do not accept new inflow of cash. New investor can invest in these funds only when existing shareholder sell her shares. So the total number of shares does not change. Trade of shares does not necessarily at NAV but can be at discount or at premium. Due to no continuous inflow and outflow of cash, managers of these funds can invest according to plan and they do not feel any pressure to search for new securities or to entertain any withdrawal request.

Load vs No-load mutual funds: Load funds charge additional fee for purchase of securities (up-front fee) or redemption fee (at time of redemption of shares) or both. These fees are charged to cover for the cost of buying, cost of holding and or sale costs of securities. On the other hand no load mutual funds do not charge any of these fee but they can charge annual management fee which is generally a percentage of NAV.

Types of mutual funds

Money market mutual funds: As the name suggests, these funds invest in short term securities. They are just like bank deposits with a very little level of extra risk. They can be taxable or tax free. Usually these funds invest in bonds with maturity of less than one year.

Bond market mutual funds: These funds invest in medium to longer term bond market (bonds having maturity of more than one year).

Stock market mutual funds: These are the most popular mutual funds. They invest in stocks. These funds can be actively or passively managed. Actively managed funds charge higher fee because their expected rate of return is higher. The passively managed funds charge lower fee while they try to earn their benchmark rate of return. The taxes are also higher for actively managed funds as there is higher turnover. Stock market funds are also called equity funds.

Hybrid funds: Hybrid or balanced funds invest in money as well as equity market.

Other pooled investments

Exchange traded funds: These are like closed-end funds except two differences. EFTs are usually passively managed while closed-end funds are usually actively managed. Closed-end funds usually trade at discount or at premium from NAV but EFTs are traded at or very close to NAV because of purchase and sales in secondary market. The investors can buy the shares of these funds in secondary market just like any other shares. Investors can receive dividends and can sale their ownership in trading hours in stock exchange only by paying brokerage commission. Investors of ETFs can involve intra-day trading and there is not up-front or redemption fee involved. The minimum investment requirement for EFTs is also very lower than mutual funds.

Commodity exchange traded funds (commodity ETFs): These are the funds that invest in physical commodities or hold derivatives of the commodities. The investors can buy the equity of these funds.

Hedge funds: These are usually limited partnerships in which the mangers are general partners and the qualified investors are limited partners. These funds apply aggressive strategies to beat the market. These funds have two fee structures; management fee and incentive fee. Use of leverage is very common characteristic of these funds.

Hedge funds are actively managed funds. Hedge funds always restrict redemption. There is a lock period before which the funds cannot be withdrawn. Funds providers have to give early notice for the funds to be withdrawn. There is always a redemption fee.

Funds of hedge funds hold the equity of many hedge funds.

Hedge funds trade through prime brokers. Prime brokers provide many services to them like custodial, administrative services, money and securities lending along with the trading services.

Benefits and Risks: Managers of hedge funds are experts and use different strategies to diversify and reduce overall risks. But the element of risk cannot be eliminated and there are risks associated with hedge funds as they are actively managed. Usually the returns of hedge funds are less correlated with other securities but the correlation tends to get higher at time of crisis.

Structure of hedge fund and fee: Hedge funds are also less regulated and less transparent. Hedge funds have two types of fee; management fee and performance fee. The management fee is necessarily to be paid to cover the operational expenditures of fund. It usually ranges from 1 to 4 percent of net assets under management. The performance fee is paid only if the performance exceeds the hurdle rate (the minimum benchmark). The incentive fee can be in between 10 to 50 percent. Some hedge funds use high water mark instead of hurdle rate. In high water mark the losses of previous period are also carried forward to check the performance of the fund.

Hedge fund valuation: The value of a hedge fund is the market value of the securities in portfolio. For liquid securities a conservative approach or average value is used. Conservative approach means we take the market price at which the securities can be immediately sold. For example bind price for buying and ask price for sale. In average approach we average the bind and ask prices. For illiquid securities a reduced price of quoted price is used (for bid and ask) to account for the illiquidity. Some funds use NAV.

High water mark: This is another fee structure of hedge funds. In this structure the incentive fee can only be paid if the net gains are crossing the hurdle rate. It means the gains which just offset the previous losses cannot be given incentive fee.

Fund of funds charge another fee structure. They charge another management fee and incentive fee (in excess of original management and performance fee).

The management fee can be calculated as beginning-period-value under management of end of period value of assets under management. The incentive fee can be calculated as net of management fee (assets under management – management fee) or independent of management fee.

Individually managed accounts/ separately managed accounts/wrap accounts: These are for high net worth investors or institutions that have their own investment goals, tax and other financial circumstances. Minimum investment requirement for these accounts is higher than any other pooled investment because these are tailor made investments exclusively for the investors. The investor is the direct owner of all securities purchased unlike mutual funds.

Private equity funds: Private equity funds are private investment vehicles which have two types of partners; General partners and limited partners.

These funds invest in private companies (not publically traded companies) or in the publically traded companies who need funds to go private. Often leverage buyouts (LBOs) are mostly major part of private equity fund portfolios.

These funds are limited partnerships like hedge funds. Committed capital is what the investors provide to the fund. Committed capital may not necessarily invested all at a time but may be draw- down over a period of time as the new investable securities are identified and added into portfolio. This drawdown period is on the discretion of manager.

<u>Fee structure:</u> The fee varies from 1 to 3 percent of committed capital. The incentive or performance fee is typically 20 percent of profit. The managers cannot get performance fee until the original capital is returned to the investors. If in

start the fund performs extremely good but in later periods the performance is less than previous periods, the incentive fee may goes beyond 20 percent. If as a whole the investors are not getting 80 percent of the total profit "claw back " provision make the manager to return the excessive performance fee.

Venture capital funds: In venture capital the investment is made in new companies who have great potential to grow if they are financed. Once the company is established it can be sold by IPOs.

Learning Module 4

Basics of Portfolio Planning and Construction

1: Describe the reasons for a written investment policy statement (IPS)

After examining the client`s investment goal, time horizon, risk tolerance, liquidity needs, tax and other obligations and circumstances the analyst write IPS (Investment policy statement). IPS contains investment objectives, constraints and a related benchmark to compare portfolio`s performance. This statement can be and should be updated as soon as investor`s circumstances change.

Without writing an IPS the investment manger cannot produce high quality results for the client. The IPS is the communication bridge between investment manager and client.

2: Describe the major components of an IPS

Every client is different, so does their IPS. A Typical IPS has following components;

- Purpose of IPS
- Identifying client`s circumstances, liquidity, tax and other obligations and source of wealth
- Investment objectives
- Risk tolerance
- Client's investment constraints
- Investment time horizon
- Duties and responsibilities of investment manager

- Duties and responsibilities of client
- Client`s familiarity with financial markets
- Special investment guidelines given by client about execution of investment, assets which can and cannot buy
- Procedure of updating IPS
- Evaluation procedure of investment and benchmark
- How to respond in different situations

Baseline strategic asset allocation rebalancing procedure

3: Describe risk and return objectives and how they may be developed for a client

Risk and return objectives are most important element of an IPS. The return objectives must be consistent with the risk and investment constraints.

Risk objectives: The risk has two factors; the client's ability and willingness to take risk. If the client has higher (lower) willingness but the ability is low (higher), it should be explained to her. The investment manager and the client must reach at a conclusion. The investment manager must not try to persuade the client to increase or decrease her willingness. If the ability to take risk is not consistent with willingness to take risk, the lower of the two must b considered.

The risk can be stated in absolute or relative terms. The absolute risk can be the probability of total loss like not more than 3% in six months. The relative risk can be attached with a benchmark like LIBOR or any index.

A relative risk can also be attached with the time an obligation will arise like a pension plan.

Return objectives: As stated before the risk and return objective must be consistent. All investors want highest return with zero risk but in practical life this is not possible. According to portfolio theory, if you want more return you must accept higher risk. Return can also be stated in absolute (like 5% p.a) or in relative terms (like track and index).

4: Explain the difference between the willingness and the ability (capacity) to take risk in analyzing an investor's financial risk tolerance

The risk has two factors; the client's ability and willingness to take risk.

The ability to take risk is a function of investment time horizon (higher time horizon means more ability), Assets vs obligations (more assets than liabilities means higher ability), having a job or not (having a secured job means more ability), expected future income (higher income means higher ability) etc.

Willingness to take risk is a function of client's attitude and believes about investment. Willingness is a very subjective term and the investment manager must take good care in judging it.

The willingness and ability to take risk must match.

If the client has higher (lower) willingness but the ability is low (higher), it should be explained to her. The investment manager and the client must reach at a conclusion. However, the investment manager must not try to persuade the client to increase or decrease to her willingness. If the ability to take risk is not consistent with willingness to take risk, the lower of the two must b considered.

5: Describe the investment constraints of liquidity, time horizon, tax concerns, legal and regulatory factors, and unique circumstances and their implications for the choice of portfolio assets

Liquidity constraints: Liquidity constraints are essential part of IPS.

Different investors/clients have different liquidity requirement at different point in time. Individual investors might have to pay for their child's college fee or to purchase a house in future. In addition to this there are several unpredicted liquidity needs like medical expenditures.

Institutional investors like insurance companies need cash to honor mostly unpredicted claims. The pension plans have mostly predicted cash needs.

The investment manager must carefully consider the liquidity requirement of the client and plan the investment accordingly. A bond can be held in portfolio maturing at same time when the cash is required is generally a good strategy.

For unpredicted liquidity requirement most liquid assets should be included in the portfolio. The hedge funds and private equity which is very illiquid investment should be avoided for high liquidity requirement.

Time horizon: Time horizon must be included in IPS. If the time horizon of an investor is short, the manager must not invest in risky assets. For longer time horizons (all other things held constant) the investment can be made in riskier and illiquid assets.

Tax concerns: The tax treatment for different investments is different. Sometimes the capital gain tax is higher than dividend or interest income. On some investments the tax can be deferred. A taxpaying investor may want to invest in tax free investments (like government securities) or in dividend paying securities. Tax concerns must also be included in IPS.

Legal and regulatory factors: Legal factors are also included in IPS. There are some general rules of financial markets. In addition to these rules there are several restrictions for individual investors. For example director of a company face restrictions to invest in his company as he may has inside information about that company. These legal and regulatory factors must be considered by investment manager.

Unique circumstances: There can be some unique investment circumstances for some investors. For example some investors do not want to invest in tobacco or alcohol providing firms. Some investors prefer not to invest in a company whose main business is on interest basis. These unique circumstances must be included in IPS.

6: Explain the specification of asset classes in relation to asset allocation

Broadly, the cash, equity, bonds and real estate are considered major asset classes. All these asset classes are traditional investments. A recent trend about investment also includes alternative investment like hedge funds, private equity, Real estate investment trusts, art etc.

All these asset classes can be subdivided into many other groups with respect to their category. For example equities can be divided with respect to issuer's size (large, small) or its geographical location (domestic company or foreign company), market liquidity (small cap or large cap), multinational or local, service sector or manufacturing sector etc. The bonds can be grouped as government bonds or corporate bonds, investable or junk bonds. There are many other ways by which these broad categories can be further divided.

After writing objectives, constraints and other circumstance in IPS we develop strategic allocation of investment in different asset classes according to liquidity needs, legal and tax circumstances, risk and return requirement etc. The correlation within an asset class must be high positive to ensure that the assets belong to each other. While the correlation between different asset classes must be low for diversification.

7: Describe the principles of portfolio construction and the role of asset allocation in relation to the IPS

After the creation of IPS and strategic allocation of assets have decided, the investment manager constructs the portfolio according to the investment objectives and risk tolerance of the investor on the efficient frontier.

While constructing the portfolio the investment manager considers the utility of investor. Utility of investor increases with increase in expected return with appropriate risk.

The investment manager (by the approval of investor) can choose tactical allocation (active management with short term deviation from the strategic allocation of assets) or passive management (strategic asset allocation) or a mix of both.

In *tactical asset allocation* the managers try to exploit a short term opportunity of earning extra return from mispriced securities which is may or may not consistent with the investment risk and return objectives.

Security selection: The investment manager try to select the securities within asset class which are best matching the investment objectives and their expected returns are higher than benchmark.

After some intervals (or when the situation changes) the portfolio should be rebalanced.

There are two famous strategies in portfolio construction; top-down approach and core-satellite approach.

In *top-down approach* many investment managers of same asset class work for the single client and mange risk. This approach generates average total return and reduces the biasness of a single manager. As they can be following same benchmark, the risk budget may be underutilized. Moreover there would be higher trading cost (due to frequent trades) and tax obligations (due to capital gains).

The core- satellite approach come up with a better solution. In this approach, major investment is made in passive management while a small portion of total investment is actively managed. The tax obligations and cost due to frequent trading can be reduced with this approach.

8: Describe how environmental, social, and governance (ESG) considerations may be integrated into portfolio planning and construction

ESG integration: While making investment decisions in companies, the investors consider these companies' impact on environment, society and governance. The responsible and cautious investors avoid all those companies which are affecting negatively (to EGG). This practice is called ESG integration into portfolio planning and construction.

ESG can be divided into following sub-categories;

Environmental issues: Like increase in pollution, contaminating water etc.

Social issues: Like child labor, gender inequality etc.

Governance issues: Like bribery, corruption etc.

For example avoiding investment in tobacco companies is a common practice.

The investors set some criteria and eliminate all those companies from the list who are using 'bad practices'. This can limit their investable asset and their overall returns might be reduces. The research on ESG and return suggests mixed results.

Learning module 5

The Behavioral Biases of Individuals

1: Compare and contrast cognitive errors and emotional biases

Irrational thoughts or actions that can influence our decision-making process (usually unconsciously) are known as behavioral biases. Behavioral biases may influence our decisions to deviate from finance theory' actual recommendations. These behavioral biases can be split into two types:

1. Cognitive errors.
2. Emotional biases

Cognitive errors: It is a systematic error in processing and interpreting the available information which eventually affects our judgement. These errors usually happens when our brain tries to simplify the available information.

Emotional bias: When we think, interpret or act on the basis of our feelings and emotions rather than facts are called Emotional biases.

2: Discuss commonly recognized behavioral biases and their implications for financial decision making

Irrational thoughts or actions that can influence our decision-making process (usually unconsciously) are known as behavioral biases. Behavioral biases may influence our decisions to deviate from finance theory' actual recommendations. These behavioral biases can be split into two types:

1. Cognitive errors.
2. Emotional biases

Cognitive errors: It is a systematic error in processing and interpreting the available information which eventually affects our judgement. These errors usually happens when our brain tries to simplify the available information.

Cognitive errors can be divided into:

i. Belief perseverance bias
ii. Processing errors

Belief perseverance bias: Also called belief persistence. Belief persistence refers to people's unwillingness to change their minds despite new information or facts that contradict or refute their ideas. To put it another way, belief perseverance refers to people's tendency to hold onto their beliefs even when they are incorrect. Belief preservation bias five sub-types;

a. Conservatism bias.
b. Confirmation bias.
c. Representativeness bias.
d. Illusion of control bias.
e. Hindsight bias.

a. *Conservatism bias:* Conservative bias is defined as holding on to old beliefs or ideas while accepting new information that contradicts or upsets those beliefs or notions with hesitancy. People have a tendency to overestimate their own prediction based on old information in general and underestimate new information. As a result, incorrect conclusions are reached and inadequate solutions to new problems are implemented.

Implications / effects of conservative biases on financial decision making: Even with the availability of new information the investor may be slow to update his investment forecast.

Sometimes investor may choose to stay with old belief rather than to deal with the stress to update his belief on the basis of new information.

For example, an investor may buy a security in an oil and gas exploration company because it has discovered some new oil wells. After a few weeks, company discloses that the newly discovered wells does not provide sufficient crude oil. If the investor sticks to his or her initial assessment of the firm and fails to adjust their assessment based on fresh facts, he is subject to conservative bias.

How to Recognize and Overcome the Conservatism Bias

- **Seek Professional Advice:** To avoid conservatism bias an investor must consult other specialists to assist them in making financial decisions. In this way the same available information can be interpreted in a different way.

- Do adequate analysis and weight the new information properly. After the deep analysis the investor should act quickly as the time is very important in investment decision making.

a. *Confirmation bias:* The propensity to appreciate or recognise information that confirm one's present ideas while dismissing evidence that contradicts them is known as confirmation bias. It happens when someone rationalises their beliefs in order to ease cognitive stress.

Implications / effects of Confirmation bias on financial decision making:

- An investor can wrongly focus on positive sides of an

investment opportunity while ignores the negative points about it.

- While just focusing on positive new the investor may under diversify the portfolio which may result as more losses than it may produces.

How to recognize and overcome the *Confirmation bias*

This bias can be mitigated by finding out the contradictory piece of information.

By analyzing the investment opportunity on the basis of different perspectives can help to reduce this bias.

c) Representative Bias: When we interpret new knowledge as a duplicate or representative of old experience. While new information may appear to be similar to previously classified information, the two sets of information may actually be completely different.

There are two types of representative bias

- Base rate neglect: The frequency of an occurrence in a wider population is neglected in favor of specific knowledge.
- Sample size neglect: In this situation, investors make the error of assuming that tiny sample sizes correctly represent populations.

Implications / effects of representative bias on financial decision making:

A Financial forecast is mostly dependent on a limited sample size or individual, unique data as a consequence of representational bias.

An investor will not tend to take stress to update the belief which will cause losses.

How to recognize and overcome the *representative bias*

Learn more about statistics and logical reasoning to avoid the representativeness bias, and ask others to point out situations where you may be focusing too much on representativeness.

d) Illusion of Control Bias: People who suffer from illusion control bias believe they can alter or control outcomes when they cannot.

Implications / effects of* Illusion of Control Bias *on financial decision making:

A false sense of control may do tremendous damage to an investor's wealth. The illusion of control leads people to invest in penny stocks. This is because they feel that because the firm is small, they can use their wealth to acquire a major share in it and thereby influence the result.

How to avoid; Diversify to reduce this risk. Look for material information that opposes your point of view. This not only reduces the appearance of control, but also prevents falling subject to another biases (i.e confirmation bias).

e) Hindsight Bias: A belief that someone has correctly predicted an event before it occurs. It leads to overconfidence in one's capacity to foresee other future occurrences.

Implications / effects of* Hindsight Bias *on financial decision making:

Because of hindsight bias, you perceive events to be more predictable than they actually are which can cause a major loss of investment.

How to Detect and overcome:

1. Remind yourself that you can't predict the future.
2. Deeply examine the data.
3. Consider alternative outcomes and list them
4. Make your decision and analyze the outcome.

Second type of cognitive error is processing error

ii. Processing error

Inappropriate, irrational and illogical processing of available information is called processing error. It has four types,

- Anchoring and adjustment bias.
- Mental accounting bias.

- Framing bias.
- Availability bias.

Anchoring and adjustment bias: Anchoring and adjustment is a cognitive bias in which a person is too reliant on the first piece of information received.

Effects: This bias can produce erroneous evaluation in investment.

How to detect and avoid: Acknowledge the bias. Slow your decision-making process and search for more information and information from more reliable source.

b) Mental Accounting Bias

Mental accounting bias refers to our tendency to divide our money into several "accounts," which influences how we think about our expenditures. We believe money to be less fungible than it is due to mental accounting.

Effects: Mental accounting commonly leads to poor investment decisions as well as inefficient or unethical financial behaviour, such as financing a low-interest savings account while owing a large credit card debt.

How to detect and avoid: Individuals should perceive money as entirely fungible when allocating across multiple accounts, whether it's a budget account or a wealth account.

c) **Framing Bias:** The concept of framing bias relates to the idea that the way data is presented may influence how people make decisions.

Effects: An investor may misconceive the risks and returns associated with a security or portfolio which can result as more losses.

How to detect and avoid: Investors should verify if their concentration is on one single position's gain or loss to uncover framing bias. Investors should avoid referring to prior wins and losses, instead focusing on future expectations, remaining impartial, and being open to fresh decision-making recommendations.

d) Availability Bias: The use of the most conveniently accessible or available information rather than that which is necessarily the most representative. It has four basic sources

i. Retrievability: Even if the initial response or concept that comes to mind is erroneous, it will most likely be regarded accurate.

ii. Resonance: The closer a scenario mirrors a person's own circumstance, the more likely they are to be biased.

iii. Categorization: People acquire information from what they think to be relevant sets of searches as they address issues.

iv. Narrow range of experience: When estimating, an individual may rely on a narrow range of experience rather than considering numerous views.

Effects: Due to tis bias, investors may only be able to operate with a limited number of investments securities from a single nation or industry.

The advertisement or news coverage may influence an investor's decision.

Which leads to under diversification of portfolio.

How to detect and overcome: Create a team with a wide range of experiences and perspectives and involve them in the decision-making process. When making judgments, make use of your network.

Emotional Biases

When we think, interpret or act on the basis of our feelings and emotions rather than facts are called Emotional biases.

There are six emotional biases

a. Loss aversion bias.
b. Overconfidence bias
c. Self-control bias
d. Status quo bias
e. Endowment bias
f. Regret aversion bias

a. **Loss aversion bias:** The practise of avoiding losses in order to maximise earnings is known as loss aversion. Rather than reducing their losses, rational investors should be willing to take on more risk in order to increase their profits. Loss aversion causes investors to hold on to losing assets to avoid losing money, while selling their profitable investments to lock in profits.

Effects:

The Investor may hold long an investment which is in loss in A hope to come up with a profit. On the other hand the investor may sell profit making investment too early.

How to detect and avoid: A systematic investment plan can help to eliminate loss aversion bias. Even if a loss is emotionally painful, a reasonable appraisal of the chances of profit and loss can help investors make better investment decisions.

a. **Overconfidence bias:** Overconfidence bias is the tendency to make erroneous and inaccurate assessments of our talents, intellect, or aptitude.

It has two further types

i. Prediction overconfidence: Prediction overconfidence refers to an investor's tendency to make overly specific predictions with a very narrow range.
ii. Certainty overconfidence: Overconfidence in one's capacity to select the next big stock with 100% certainty (or higher probability) is known as certainty overconfidence.

Effects: Overconfident investors may overestimate expected gains while underestimating potential risks.

Investors may opt to invest their money into poorly diversified portfolios, placing themselves at risk of losing a large sum of money.

<u>How to detect and avoid:</u> Consider the ramifications. Consider the repercussions while making a decision. Challenge yourself while assessing your abilities. Maintain an open mind. Consider your blunders and never ignore them. Pay attention to what others have to say.

c) Self-Control Bias: When people prioritize instant gratification above long-term goals, they develop self-control bias. It's an emotional human-behavioral tendency in which people fail to act in pursuit of their long-term overall goals owing to a lack of self-control in the short term.

Effects: As a result of investor's incapacity to save for the future, investors may take on excessive stock market risk and borrow too much money on even higher rates in order to generate higher returns.

Self-control bias may result in an asset allocation mismatch, as well as investors losing sight of basic financial principles.

How to detect and avoid: Investors should be disciplined, should make personal budgets and plan the investments. These plans must be evaluated on a regular intervals.

d) Status Quo Bias: People affected by this bias desire to the things to stay the same or that the current state of affairs remain the same even when the change is necessary.

Effects: When presented with a critical decision, investors are more likely to pick the option that maintains the status quo. It inhibits investor from perceiving potential benefits that outweigh the risks or sometimes the risk profile of the existing opportunities has changed but the investor do not want to change her portfolio.

How to detect and avoid: Proper portfolio diversification and asset allocation while minimization of risk can reduce the probability of this bias.

e) Endowment Bias: It is cognitive bias that encourages people to appreciate an owned security more than its market value.

Effects: Investors may fail or be hesitant to sell some assets and replace them with others which can result into sub-optimal asset allocation.

How to detect and avoid: Avoid emotional attachment to a certain security and make evaluate them according to the market.

f) Regret-aversion Bias: Inability of an investor to make a decision for the fear of being wrong and which will lead toward regret.

Effects: A regret-aversion bias can cause the investor to avoid self-decision and follow the herd. Investors may also invest in least risky assets to avoid the regret which will result in not fulfilment of investment goals.

How to detect and avoid:

Diversification: Risk avoidance is at the heart of regret aversion bias. Diversification can reduce the risk.

Second, it is critical for stock investors to have a long-term approach to their investments.

3: Describe how behavioral biases of investors can lead to market characteristics that may not be explained by traditional finance

Sometime the behavioral biases can lead the market to certain patterns called market anomalies.

Market anomaly

It is a situation in which a security or a group of securities do not reflect all the current relevant available information. A market anomaly means some securities are not following efficient market hypothesis. This anomaly should be for longer period of time. A deviation from common rule for shorter period could exist in less efficient markets. Market anomalies can be grouped as time series, cross sectional, and others.

Anomalies in time series data

Calendar anomalies: Anomalies linked with different days, months or years are called calendar anomalies. The most common calendar anomaly is January effect. In January the stock tend to perform very well. This performance can be explained as the fund managers tend to sell securities in December and buy them in January for the taxation issues or to show better financial results in December. Other calendar anomalies are weekend effect, turn-of-the month effect, and turn-of-the-year effect.

Momentum and overreaction anomalies: Momentum anomaly occurs when an asset's price rises (falls) it pushes the price to rise (fall) further. Overreaction anomaly is when a security has performed poorly in three to five years (3 to 5 is not a hard and fast rule), will perform better in coming years due to cognitive biasness (behavioral finance).

Cross-Sectional Anomalies

Size effect: **It states that small companies have higher returns than larger companies or small-cap companies outperform the large-cap companies. In literature this effect existed until 1980s. It is**

argued that this was a random statistical result and does not actually exist.

Value effect: It is an anomaly that the companies which are being traded at lower P/E, Market to Book value ratios and higher dividend yield (value stocks) had outperformed the growth stock (with higher P/E, Market to Book value ratios and lower dividend yield). These stocks attract the value investors and they can drag the price up.

Other Anomalies

Closed-ended funds: Sometimes closed ended funds are being traded at a discount from their NAV. Future expectations about manager's performance, tax inefficiencies and transaction costs can explain these anomalies partially.

Earnings surprises: When stock price does not adjust to an unexpected announcement at-least at the same day. The traders can exploit this opportunity.

IPOs: IPOs are generally underpriced and the buyers of such stocks can earn excessive return. Sometimes the buyers drag the prices too higher than the actual price.

Most of the time these anomalies are result of statistical methods in use and overreaction/under-reaction of investors so trading based on these anomalies could not be always profitable.

Leaning Module 6
Introduction to Risk Management

1: Define risk management.

Risk can be defined in a single word as 'uncertainty'. When the future outcome of an investment is not 100 percent certain it is called risky investment. Almost a certain level of risk is involved to all of our activities including investment. The individual investors and institutions can reduce the risk that is called risk management.

The institutes can reduce the risk by identifying the risk, calculating their risk tolerance, choosing which and how much risk they can take and transferring the risk to another party (i.e. insurance companies).

Individuals can also reduce the risk by not investing in junk securities, diversifying and using insurance products.

All those process to reduce the risk is called risk management.

2: Describe features of a risk management framework.

Every organization faces risk especially the firms in investment industry. Actually firms benefit from risk because without risk there is no reward. The firms create a framework to manage risk so they can balance the risk and return. Effective risk management increases the credibility of firms, giving them more access to low cost capital. Investors do prefer the firms that have effective risk management framework.

A good risk management framework must have following features;

- A process to identify risk
- Process and policies for risk governance
- Risk measurement and risk tolerance of the firm
- Minimizing risk
- Reporting and monitoring of risk

3: Define risk governance and describe elements of effective risk governance.

It is a top to down process. The governing body of a firm defines risk goals of the firm and identifies the risk tolerance. They risk management team decides which risks they can take, the risks they can reduces and the risks they should be avoiding. Then a process is established to ensure that each and every employee is performing his/her duties in consistent to risk management framework. The role of employees is defined and authorities are assigned to monitor and for approvals of different employees actions.

4: Explain how risk tolerance affects risk management.

As we know that every firm has to take a certain level of risk in order to achieve its goals. The risk tolerance is the firm`s ability to withstand in case of losses. The firm can face internal as well external risks.

The risk tolerance can be a function of

- The firm`s ability to respond a certain bad event
- Firm`s ability to stay undamaged in losses
- Firm`s competitive environment
- Regulatory environment

The risk management team can determine types of risk the firm can take, can be reduced and those which should be avoided, in determining the risk tolerance of the firm. Only those risks should be accepted which give better reward and are consistent with firm`s goals.

5: Describe risk budgeting and its role in risk governance.

After determining risk tolerance there comes risk budgeting. In risk budgeting we allocate all of our investment in different assets. The aggregate risk of these assets must be equal to our risk tolerance level.

In this way we choose all those investable assets which give us maximum return within our risk budget.

We can budget our risk using a single measure or by using multi-dimensional measures

Following are the most common single measure being used for portfolio risk budgeting;

- Standard deviation
- Downside standard deviation
- Value at risk
- Beta
- Portfolio duration

For multi-dimensional measures, factor analysis is most common. In factor analysis, different factors (interest rate, exchange rate etc) are analyzed how much they can affect different asset classes.

Some common risk budgeting practices are

Limit the beta to 0.90

Allocate 90% of portfolio in government securities and 10% in corporate bonds

Allocate the investment in those assets which can be least affected by interest rate change.

6: Identify financial and non-financial sources of risk and describe how they may interact.

Financial risks are related to financial market like unfavorable market movement or share price movement. Non-financial risks are risks which are not related to financial market. The source of non-financial risk can be within an organization or outside of the organization (but not from the financial market).

Financial Risks

Market risk: The unfavorable movement of share price, a downfall of overall market, changes in interest rate etc.

Credit risk: Risk of default of counterparty.

Liquidity risk: The risk that the firm will not be able to sell an asset at a fair price. This usually happens in a stressful market or when the underlying asset has less liquid market.

Non-financial risks

Legal risk: Risk that counterparty will sue you.

Compliance risk: Risk that an organization will not meet the regulatory requirement. This also involves un-ability to meet recent changes in taxation laws, accounting disclosure requirement etc.

Model risk: Risk of using un-appropriate model for security evaluation.

Tail risk: Risk that an extreme event will occur which will affect the organization in a bad way. The returns on financial markets do not follow normal distribution. There are usually "fat tails".

Solvency risk: Risk that the company will be defaulted.

Operational risk: The risk that the employees of an organization can make errors which can cost the organization.

Political risk: Risk that the government`s policies will change.

All these risks interact with each other. The total risk might be bigger than the sum of all these risks.

For example, suppose a big customer failed to pay the services he has taken from the organization. Due to a customer`s default, our firm may not have enough cash to pay its suppliers and employees. Some employees can be fired which sued the firm and there is legal risk.

7: Describe methods for measuring and modifying risk exposures and factors to consider in choosing among the methods.

Most common risk measures are as follows;

Standard deviation: It measures the volatility of returns. It is most common measure of risk when the distribution of returns is normal. In financial markets the outcomes do not generally show normal distribution. This measure is not good for negatively skewed or fat tailed distributions.

Beta: It measures the systematic or market risk. This measure assumes diversification so it is good for portfolio.

Duration: It measures the sensitivity of debt securities (fixed income) to change in interest rate.

Value at risk (VaR): It measures the risk of loss on an investment. It tells us minimum losses over a specific period with a given probability in normal business conditions. This method is being widely used by investment and commercial banks.

For example an investment firm has VaR of $2 million with a probability of 1% in a week. It means that the chances of losing $2million in a week are 2%.

Drawbacks of VaR: It does not tell us maximum losses.

It uses normal distribution which is the rare case in financial markets.

It can be manipulated by using most stable periods.

Critics claims that VaR usually understate the actual situation.

Due to all above drawbacks VaR should be used along with other risk measures.

We have a better modified value at risk model called

Conditional value at risk (CVaR): Also called expected shortfall. It uses the weighted average of tails of a distribution. Due to this the CVaR goes beyond the VaR. It is more conservative approach to measure the value at risk.

When the expected outcomes are stable, the normal VaR is sufficient. But with more volatile expected outcomes, we need to use CVaR.

The derivative risk measures

They are also called "the Greeks". They are used to measure the derivative risks.

Delta (Δ): It is the value sensitivity of a derivative to change in the price of underlying asset.

Δ = Change in price of derivative ÷ Change in price of underlying asset

For example if Δ for an option is 0.5, it means if the price of underlying moves by $1 the option price will change by $0.5 in same direction (due to positive sign of delta).

Theta (θ): It tells us how much the value of an option will fall as the time to expiration decreases. Theta is expressed as daily decline in value and its value is generally negative.

Gamma (Γ): It is the rate of change in Delta if the price of underlying asset changes. Higher Gamma shows higher sensitivity of derivative to its underlying.

Vega: It measures the rate of change in price of derivative in response to change in volatility of underlying asset.

Rho: It tells us the rate of change in derivative price when the interest rate changes.

Subjective risk measures

Scenario analysis: In scenario analysis we use different scenarios and see what can happen to our portfolio in those scenarios. Scenario analysis does not tell us a single Value but different outcomes under different scenarios.

For example we can see what worst can happen to our investment if the interest rate increases along with exchange rate movement.

Stress testing: In stress testing we take extreme cases (like market crisis etc) and see what will happen to our investment.

Modifying risk

Modifying risk does not necessarily means avoiding the risk. It means rebalancing the risk. Some risks can be accepted while others can be reduced and avoided.

The goal of risk modification is taking optimal level of risks.

Risks can be avoided by not taking part in those activities. If the expected returns of a security are highly volatile, the investor can avoid it. The securities which have crossed a border line of a certain level of risk can be reduced from a portfolio and the other securities of fewer risk characteristics can be added.

Some risks can be prevented. For example operational and compliance risks can be prevented by enforcing strong procedures and systems.

Some risks must be accepted to achieve organization`s goals like investment risk.

Some risks can be transferred to insurance companies.

Risks can also be shifted. Shifting can be done by the use of hedging in derivative market.

Choosing a modification method

The method of risk modification should be adopted by considering cost-benefit analysis. Usually the companies use a mix of differ modification methods.

For example banks heavily depend on insurances but they also use hedging.

Don't miss out!

Visit the website below and you can sign up to receive emails whenever M. Imran Ahsan publishes a new book. There's no charge and no obligation.

https://books2read.com/r/B-A-ZWUK-BGIZE

Connecting independent readers to independent writers.

Did you love *CFA 2026 level 1: Portfolio management*? Then you should read *CFA 2026 Level 1: Fixed Income*[1] by Dr. M. Imran Ahsan!

[2]

If you want to learn CFA easily and with less time, you have the right book. If you think Fixed income is diffcult, just read this book. It will change your perception.

Many books are available in the market for the same purpose and they are good. The main quality of this book which distinguishes it from others is this book covers whole syllabus in very precise and comprehensive manner. This book makes difficult concepts easy and understandable.

We believe in simplicity and conciseness. This book is a complete and a comprehensive guide with simple language.

---

1. https://books2read.com/u/4NL1RW

2. https://books2read.com/u/4NL1RW

You can learn the complete Fixed Income material in just one week with the help of this book.

Also by M. Imran Ahsan

ACCA

ACCA: Business & Technology

CFA level 1

CFA 2026: Level 1 corporate Issuers

CFA 2026: Level 1 Financial Statement Analysis

CFA level 1: 2026 Equity Investments

CFA 2026 LEVEL 1: Economics

CFA 2026 Level 1: Derivatives and Alternative Investments

CFA 2026 level 1: Portfolio management

Investment series

Corporate Finance: A Beginner's Guide

Fixed Income Securities: A Beginner's Guide to Understand, Invest and Evaluate Fixed Income Securities

Personal Finance

Side Hustle Success: Unlock Your Earning Potential

About the Author

I am a PhD scholar and is a university lecturer for more than 11 years. I have been teaching Finance and Economics at various levels.

As an instructor I believe in simplicity, comprehensivity and in conciseness. I believe in smart kind of hard work. It means you should use your time efficiently to achieve optimal goals with limited time and efforts.

www.ingramcontent.com/pod-product-compliance
Lightning Source LLC
LaVergne TN
LVHW022024200926
848481LV00007B/2528